The Trouble With Love
(and other cases of mistaken identity)

a comedy of manners in two acts

by

Ronnie Meek

WordCrafts Theatrical

WordCrafts Theatrical Press
The Trouble With Love
(and other cases of mistaken identity)
Copyright © 2019, Ronnie Meek
All Rights Reserved

CAUTION: Professionals and amateurs are hereby warned that performance of *The Trouble With Love (and other cases of mistaken identity)* is subject to payment of a royalty. It is fully protected under the copyright laws of the United States of America, and of all countries covered by the International Copyright Union. All rights, including professional, amateur, motion picture, public reading, broadcast, and any other reproduction by means known or yet to be discovered are strictly reserved.

All rights are controlled exclusively by WordCrafts Theatrical Press, 912 East Lincoln Street, Tullahoma, Tennessee 37388. No performance of this play may be given without obtaining in advance the written permission of WordCrafts Theatrical Press, https://www.wordcrafts.net/performance-rights-request, and paying the requisite fee.

SPECIAL NOTE

Anyone receiving permission to produce *The Trouble With Love (and other cases of mistaken identity)* is required to give credit to the Author as the sole and exclusive Author of the Play on the title page of all programs distributed in connection with performances of the Play and in all instances in which the title of the Play appears for purposes of advertising, publicizing or otherwise exploiting the Play. The name of the Author must appear on a separate line, in which no other name appears, immediately beneath the title and in size of type equal to 50% of the size of the largest, most prominent letter used for the title of the Play. No person, firm or entity may receive credit larger or more prominent than that accorded the Author.

All rights reserved. No part of this book may be reproduced, stored in a retrieval system, or transmitted in any form or by any means—electronic, mechanical, photocopy, recording, or otherwise—without the prior written permission of the publisher. The only exception is brief quotations for review purposes.

Published by WordCrafts Theatrical Press
912 E. Lincoln St. Tullahoma, Tennessee 37388
www.wordcrafts.net

The Trouble With Love (and other cases of mistaken identity) is based upon the original stage play, *She Stoops to Conquer*, a comedy by Oliver Goldsmith, which was first performed in London in 1773.

CAST

Mrs. Dorothy Hardcastle
Horace Hardcastle
Tony Lumpkin
Miss Kate Hardcastle
Miss Constance Neville
Henry Hastings
Charles Marlowe Jr
David Diggory
Sir Charles Marlowe Sr

Tavern Patrons
  Dick
  Jack
  Sally
  Tom
  Landlord
Servants (may be doubled from Tavern Patrons)
  Diggory
  Roger
  Bridget, the cook-maid

ACT 1
Scene 1

The House

DOROTHY: Honestly, Horace, sometimes you are such a fuddy duddy. We are the only people we know who never go away for a holiday. We don't even go into the city. Even our two old neighbors Miss Hogg and Miss Grigsby just returned from a trip to the islands.

HARDCASTLE: Yes, and look at them! Two old biddies romping around on the beach. It will take them weeks to begin acting their age again, not to mention returning to a natural skin color. Back in my day people knew how to behave.

DOROTHY: Oh yes, we hear about "back in your day" everyday, but that doesn't mean we have to live there. Look at this old house! We are so far out in the country that we have no visitors. We are practically cut off from the world.

HARDCASTLE: And I love it. I love everything that's old: old friends, old times, old manners, old books, old wine, and I believe, Dorothy, you'll have to agree I'm pretty fond of an old wife.

DOROTHY: And since when is 40 considered old?

HARDCASTLE: Well 40 isn't old… unless you add 17 to it.

DOROTHY: And why would anyone do that? My dear sweet Tony has not yet reached his maturity.

HARDCASTLE: No, he hasn't, but not for lack of years.

DOROTHY: No matter. Tony has a good fortune waiting for him.

HARDCASTLE: He's going to need it. He has little enough education.

DOROTHY: One doesn't need to know anything when one has enough money.

HARDCASTLE: You may have something there. Still, it wouldn't hurt to know a bit about how to behave.

DOROTHY: My Tony's behavior is perfect. He simply has a sense of humor.

HARDCASTLE: Sense of humor? If you call burning the gardener's shoes, and scaring the maid, and leaving open the gate to the pig sty a sense of humor then he certainly has one alright.

DOROTHY: Don't be so hard on the boy. Poor Tony was always so sickly I really couldn't send him to school, but once he gets stronger perhaps he can go to law school.

HARDCASTLE: Law school! Law school? Not unless they move law school to the alehouse, or perhaps a few other places not to be mentioned.

DOROTHY: We mustn't be too hard on the poor boy. I'm not sure how long we shall have him with us. Anyone can see that he... that he is in frail and declining health.

HARDCASTLE: That's true, if growing too fat is one of the symptoms.

DOROTHY: He coughs sometimes.

HARDCASTLE: When the ale goes down the wrong way.

DOROTHY: I'm actually afraid of his lungs.

HARDCASTLE: So am I. He sometimes whoops so loudly I'm scared my eardrums will burst. (*TONY whoops in the background.*) Ah! There he is now, the poor frail fellow.

(Enter TONY.)

DOROTHY: Tony, where are you going my charmer? Please sit for awhile and visit your papa and me.

Tony: I'm in haste, mother, I cannot stay!

Dorothy: Oh no, my dearest. The weather is far too raw today. Poor Tony, you don't look at all well.

Tony: I can't stay, I tell you. The Three Pigeons is expecting me this very moment. There's fun to be had!

Hardcastle: Law school indeed!

Dorothy: But Tony, that's a low crowd at the Three Pigeons.

Tony: Not at all Mother. There is Dick Muggins the pig farmer. Jack Slang the teamster. Little Sally who plays the music box. And Tom Twist. He does card tricks.

Dorothy: Please Tony, disappoint them just this once.

Tony: Ah mother, I'm not worried about disappointing them. It's myself I can't stand to disappoint.

Dorothy: You shall not go! (*She grabs hold of him.*)

Tony: I will, I tell you!

Dorothy: I say, "no."

Tony: We'll see who's stronger, you or I. (*TONY exits hauling DOROTHY with him.*)

Hardcastle: If ever a pair was well met it is those two. Ah! And here comes my own daughter Kate. (*KATE enters.*) Good morning, my dear. I see you are dressed out in the height of fashion today.

Kate: You know our agreement, father. You allow me the morning to go about my business dressed as I like and in the evening I dress plainly to please you.

Hardcastle: I certainly do, and I believe this evening will be a test of how well you hold to our agreement.

Kate: What do you mean?

Hardcastle: I expect that we shall receive a visit this evening from the young man I have chosen to be your husband. I have his father's letter telling me that his son is to come today and the father shall follow shortly after.

KATE: Really, I wish I had known before. This is likely to be so formal and cold it's a thousand-to-one that I won't like him.

HARDCASTLE: Don't be so sure. I'll never force your choice, but he is the son of my old friend Sir Charles Marlowe. He is said to be a first class scholar. He has an excellent position awaiting him. And he is reputed to be of excellent character.

KATE: (*Intrigued*) Is he?

HARDCASTLE: Also, very generous.

KATE: It's possible I might like him.

HARDCASTLE: Young and brave.

KATE: I think I could probably like him.

HARDCASTLE: Oh, I'm also told he's very handsome.

KATE: My dear Papa, say no more. I'll have him!

HARDCASTLE: And to crown all, Kate, he's one of the most reserved and bashful fellows in all the world.

KATE: Eh! Papa, reserved? I've always heard that a reserved lover makes a suspicious husband.

HARDCASTLE: Surely not. Modesty is a crowning virtue. That was perhaps the main thing that recommended him to me.

KATE: It doesn't recommend him to me. However, if everything else you have said proves true he may still do. I think I'll have him.

HARDCASTLE: Yes, well there is still the question of whether he will have you.

KATE: What! Well, if he refuses that will be his loss. I'll not pine away. I'll simply say, "Good riddance," and end up with someone better.

HARDCASTLE: That's the spirit, my girl. Well, I'm off to address the servants. We so seldom receive guests that the servants will need a bit of instruction in how to act. (*Exit*)

KATE: Well this is some news. Young, handsome, sensible, good natured, I like all of that. But then reserved and bashful? Maybe he could be cured of those faults by the right wife? Yes, well, I'm trying to change the husband before I've secured the lover.

(Enter CONSTANCE.)

KATE: Constance, tell me, how do I look today? My face? My hair? Is this a good day? Bad day? What?

CONSTANCE: You look perfect, my dear. What is all of this about? Something's up. I can tell.

KATE: I have just been threatened with a lover.

CONSTANCE: Really? Do we know this lover's name?

KATE: Marlowe, the son of Sir Charles Marlowe.

CONSTANCE: No! He just happens to be the best friend of my Mr. Hastings. They are always together. Surely you have seen him before.

KATE: Never.

CONSTANCE: He is… unique. When he is around women of reputation and virtue he is amazingly modest, but his friends say that when he is around other types of women he is quite… different. If you catch what I mean.

KATE: Different?

CONSTANCE: Yes.

KATE: We'll just have to see how it all goes. Speaking of your Mr. Hastings, is my mother still trying to pair you up with my brother Tony?

CONSTANCE: She is always telling me such glowing wonderful things about her sweet delightful monster.

KATE: She actually believes those things. And, she has no intention of letting a fortune such as yours leave the family.

CONSTANCE: My "fortune" is basically all in jewels and not very useful. If Hastings will just be patient I'm sure I can wait her out. In the meantime it is best to let her think I am interested in Tony.

KATE: At least Tony is your ally. I could almost love him for hating you so.

CONSTANCE: Tony is actually good-natured at heart, and I'm sure he wants to see me married… to anyone but himself.

Scene 2

The Three Pigeons

DICK: Quiet now, everyone. The young squire Tony Lumpkin is going to sing us all a song.

ALL: Yea! Hear hear! Hurrah!

JACK: Quiet! Quiet now, hear him.

TONY: *Our parlour wanted papering*
And Pa says it was waste
To call the paperhangers in
And so he made some paste
He got some rolls of paper
A ladder and a brush
And with me Mother's nightgown on
At it he made a rush, Oh!

ALL: When *Papa papered the parlour*
You couldn't see Pa for paste
Dabbing it here and dabbing it there
There was paste and paper everywhere
Mother was stuck to the ceiling
And the kids were stuck to the floor
You never saw such a bloomin' stuck up family before.
Ai Da da dum dee dee dee di dum
Da da dum dee dee dee di dum

TONY: *Pa fell off the ladder*
And dropped the paper hanger's can

> *On little sister Mary*
> *Sitting there with her young man.*
> *He stuck them both together*
> *To keep it all polite*
> *We had to call the parson in*
> *To make them man and wife. Oh!*

ALL: *When Papa papered the parlour*
> *You couldn't see Pa for paste*
> *Dabbing it here and dabbing it there*
> *There was paste and paper everywhere*
> *Mother was stuck to the ceiling*
> *And the kids were stuck to the floor*
> *You never saw such a bloomin' stuck up family before.*
> *Ai Da da dum dee dee dee di dum*
> *Da da dum dee dee dee di dum*

TONY: *We're never going to move away*
> *From that house any more*
> *For Father's gone and stuck the chairs*
> *And the tables to the floor*
> *We can't find our piano*
> *Though it's broad and rather tall*
> *We think that it's behind the paper*
> *Pa stuck on the wall. Oh!*

ALL: *When Papa papered the parlour*
> *You couldn't see Pa for paste*
> *Dabbing it here and dabbing it there*
> *There was paste and paper everywhere*
> *Mother was stuck to the ceiling*
> *And the kids were stuck to the floor*
> *You never saw such a bloomin' stuck up family before.*

(Cheers)

DICK: The squire's got spunk in him.

JACK: I love to hear him sing. His songs are always so uplifting, never low.

SALLY: I can't bear anything low.

TOM: The genteel thing is the genteel thing anytime.

JACK: That is quite a proverb you've come up with, Tom.

DICK: What a pity it is the squire is not come to his own fortune. It would be well for all the pub owners within ten miles round of him.

TONY: So it would, Master Dick, the pub owners and my friends as well.

JACK: O he takes after his own father for that. To be sure old Squire Lumpkin was the finest gentleman I ever set my eyes on.

TONY: When I'm of age I'll be just like him.

(Enter LANDLORD)

LANDLORD: There be two gentlemen in a carriage at the door. They've lost their way through the forest; and they are talking something about Mr. Hardcastle.

TONY: I'm sure one of them is the gentleman come down from London to court my sister.

LANDLORD: Aye, they look like a couple of dandies from London.

TONY: Have them come to me. I'll set them on the straight course. (*LANDLORD exits.*) Gentlemen, these two may not be quite up to your standards. If you'll retire to the next room I'll be with you in the shake of a lamb's tail. (*Mob exits.*) Mr. Hardcastle has been calling me *boy* and *pup* for the last six months. Now is my chance for revenge.

(Enter MARLOWE and HASTINGS.)

MARLOWE: What a tedious uncomfortable day have we had of it! We were told it was forty miles across the country, and we have already come over sixty.

HASTINGS: Yes, and all because you are too reserved to allow us to stop and ask directions.

MARLOWE: It's true that I am unwilling to put myself in the debt of everyone I meet. Besides, there is also the risk that one may receive an unmannerly answer.

HASTINGS: Yes, well currently we have no answer at all. We are lost!

TONY: Excuse me, gentlemen, but I understand you are inquiring about a Mr. Hardcastle. May I ask, do you have any idea where you are?

HASTINGS: None whatsoever. We should be thankful for any assistance.

Tony: Do you know the way you came?

HASTINGS: I'm afraid we are completely turned around and know nothing.

TONY: Ah, so, it seems you have lost your way.

MARLOWE: (*To HASTINGS.*) Unmannerly answer.

TONY: Pray, gentlemen, is not this same Hardcastle an old-fashioned, whimsical fellow, with an ugly face, a daughter, and a pretty son?

HASTINGS: We have not seen the gentleman; but he has the family you mention.

TONY: The daughter, a trapesing, trolloping, talkative maypole; the son, a pretty, well-bred, agreeable youth, that everybody is fond of?

MARLOWE: Our information differs in this. The daughter is said to be well-bred and beautiful; the son an awkward booby, tied at his mother's apron-string.

TONY: Then, gentlemen, all I have to tell you is, that you won't reach Mr. Hardcastle's house this night. It's a long, dark, boggy, dirty, dangerous way. Pray, sir, tell the gentlemen the way to Mr. Hardcastle's! (*Winking upon the LANDLORD.*) Mr. Hardcastle's, of Quagmire Marsh, you understand me.

LANDLORD: Master Hardcastle's! You're come a deadly deal wrong! When you came to the bottom of the hill, you should have crossed down Squash Lane.

MARLOWE: Cross down Squash Lane.

LANDLORD: Then you were to keep straight forward, till you came to four roads.

MARLOWE: Come to where four roads meet.

TONY: But you must be sure to only take one of them! Then keeping to the right, you are to go sideways till you come upon Crackskull Common: there you must look sharp for the track of the wheel, and go forward till you come to farmer Murrain's barn. Coming to the farmer's barn, you are to turn to the right, and then to the left, and then to the right about again, till you find the old mill...

MARLOWE: Wait! We could as soon find out the longitude!

HASTINGS: What's to be done, Marlowe?

MARLOWE: Perhaps the landlord can accommodate us?

LANDLORD: Sorry, master, we have but one spare bed in the whole house.

TONY: And to my knowledge, that's taken up by three lodgers already. (*After a pause, in which the rest seem disconcerted*) I have hit it. What if you go on a mile further, to the Buck's Head? The old Buck's Head on the hill is one of the best inns in the whole county.

HASTINGS: That's perfect!

LANDLORD: (*Aside to TONY*) You aren't sending them to your stepfather's house as an inn are you?

TONY: Hush! (*To HASTINGS and MARLOWE*) You have only to keep on straight forward, till you come to a large old house by the road side. You'll see a pair of large horns over the door. That's the sign. Drive up the yard, and call out stoutly.

HASTINGS: Sir, we are obliged to you.

TONY: But I do warn you, though, the landlord is rich. He wants to be thought a gentleman. He'll want to give you his company; and if you let him, he'll persuade you that his mother was an alderman, and his aunt a justice of the peace.

LANDLORD: A troublesome old blade, to be sure; but he keeps as good wines and beds as any in the whole country.

MARLOWE: Done then! We are to turn to the right, did you say?

TONY: No, no; straight forward. I'll step out myself, and show you a piece of the way. (*Smiles at the LANDLORD as all exit.*)

Scene 3

The House. Enter HARDCASTLE followed by DIGGORY, ROGER, AND BRIDGET.

HARDCASTLE: Let's see how you are in the table exercise I have been teaching you these three days. You all know your posts and your places.

ALL: Aye. Aye.

HARDCASTLE: When company comes you are not to pop out and stare, and then run in again, like frightened rabbits.

ALL: No. No.

HARDCASTLE: I have confidence in you all. You, Diggory, whom I have taken from the barn, are to stand here at the side-table; and you, Roger, whom I have advanced from the plough, are to place yourself behind my chair. But you're not to stand with your hands in your pockets. Take your hands from your pockets, Roger; and from your head. See how Diggory carries his hands. They're a little too stiff, but that's no great matter.

DIGGORY: I learned to hold my hands this way when I was drilling for the militia. And so being upon drilling…

HARDCASTLE: You must not be so talkative, Diggory. All attention must be on the guests. You must hear us talk, and not think of talking; you must see us drink, and not think of drinking; you must see us eat, and not think of eating.

DIGGORY: Begging pardon, your worship, that's perfectly unpossible. Whenever Diggory sees eating going forward he's always wishing for a mouthful himself.

HARDCASTLE: There is plenty of food in the kitchen. Just remember that you can eat in the kitchen.

DIGGORY: I thank your worship, I'll be sure to say to my stomach that a slice of cold beef is waiting in the pantry.

HARDCASTLE: Diggory, you are too talkative.—Now, if I happen to tell a good story at table, you must not all burst out a-laughing, as if you were part of the company.

DIGGORY: Then your worship must not tell the story of Old Grouse in the gun-room: I can't help laughing at that—he! he! he!—for the soul of me. We have laughed at that these twenty years—ha! ha! ha!

HARDCASTLE: (*Laughing*) That story is a good one. Well, honest Diggory, you may laugh at that—but still remember to be attentive. Suppose one of the company should call for a glass of wine, how will you behave? A glass of wine, sir, if you please (to DIGGORY).—Eh, why don't you move?

DIGGORY: But, your worship, I'm to stand here by the table.

HARDCASTLE: Will no-one move?

DIGGORY: I'm not to leave this place.

ROGER: Nor, I.

BRIDGET: I'm sure it's no place of mine.

HARDCASTLE: You numskulls! The guests will be starved. O you dunces! I must begin all over again… But wait! I hear a coach drive into the yard. To your posts, you blockheads.

I'll go and give my old friend's son a hearty reception at the gate. (*Exit.*)

DIGGORY: Blimey, my place has gone right out of my head.
BRIDGET: My place is to be everywhere.
ROGER: Does anyone know my place?
DIGGORY: My place is to be nowhere at all; and so I'm going about my business. (*All exit.*)

(*HASTINGS and MARLOWE enter.*)

HASTINGS: After the disappointments of the day, Charles, welcome at last to the comforts of a clean room and a good fire. Upon my word, a very good looking house; antique but creditable.

MARLOWE: That's what happens to these large old houses. First the owner is ruined with the upkeep and then it is turned into an inn to raise some funds.

HASTINGS: Then it is up to us travelers to foot the bill.

MARLOWE: Travelers, George, must pay in all places. In good inns you pay for luxuries. In bad inns you are simply fleeced and starved.

HASTINGS: You have spent enough time at inns. I am surprised that you are still so lacking in social confidence.

MARLOWE: Where could I have learned social confidence? My life has been chiefly spent in a college or an inn, away from the sort of women that teach men confidence. I don't know that I was ever actually acquainted with a single modest woman—except my mother.—But among females of another class, you know…

HASTINGS: I know. Among them you are forward enough. But in the company of women of reputation you look for all the world as if you want to run out of the room.

MARLOWE: Why, man, that's because I do want to run out of the room. A single glance from a pair of fine eyes and

I'm undone. A forward fellow may pretend modesty; but I'll be hanged if a modest man can ever pretend impudence.

HASTINGS: If you could say half the fine things to them that I have heard you lavish upon the barmaid, or even a cook.

MARLOWE: I can't say fine things to them; they freeze me, they petrify me. Others may fear battle, or storm, but, to me, a modest woman, dressed out in all her finery, is the most fearful object of the whole creation.

HASTINGS: How then can you ever expect to marry?

MARLOWE: Impossible! To go through all the terrors of a formal courtship meeting aunts, grandmothers, and cousins, and at last to blurt out the question, "Madam, will you marry me?" No, no, that's a strain much above me, I assure you.

HASTINGS: I pity you. How do you intend behaving to the lady you have come down to visit at the request of your father?

MARLOWE: As I behave to all other ladies. Bow very low, answer yes or no to all her demands—But then, I don't think I shall venture to look in her face. My dear Hastings, my chief reason in coming on this adventure was friendship; forwarding your happiness, not my own. Miss Neville loves you, the family doesn't know you, but as my friend you are sure of a good reception.

HASTINGS: Thank you. Were I simply trying to carry off a fortune, you should be the last man in the world I would seek for assistance. But Miss Neville's person is all I ask. Her deceased father had given his consent, and it's her desire as well.

MARLOWE: Ah! Here this fellow comes to interrupt us.

(HARDCASTLE enters followed by ROGER)

HARDCASTLE: Gentlemen, a heartily welcome. Which is Mr. Marlowe? Sir, you are heartily welcome.

MARLOWE: We thank you for your hospitality, sir.

HARDCASTLE: You'll use no ceremony in this house. Mr. Marlow—Mr. Hastings—gentlemen—pray be under no constraint in this house. This is Liberty-hall, gentlemen. Here you may do just as you please.

MARLOWE: Well, this is certainly a very nice retreat you have here.

HARDCASTLE: To hear you talking of a retreat, Mr. Marlowe, puts me in mind of the Duke of Marlborough, when we went to besiege Denain. He first summoned the garrison which consist of about five thousand men, well appointed with stores, ammunition, and other implements of war. Now, the Duke of Marlborough says to George Brooks, that stood next to him, "I'll pawn my dukedom, but I take that garrison without spilling a drop of blood." So...

MARLOWE: My good friend, if you gave us a glass of punch, it would help us to carry on the siege with vigour.

HARDCASTLE: Punch, sir!

MARLOWE: Yes, sir, punch. A glass of punch, after our journey, would be smashing. This is Liberty-hall, you know.

HARDCASTLE: I have something here a bit better, sir.

MARLOWE: (*To HASTINGS.*) So this fellow, in his Liberty-hall, will only let us have just what he pleases.

HARDCASTLE: (*Taking the cup.*) I have prepared it with my own hands, and I believe you'll agree the ingredients are tolerable. A toast, sir! Here is to our better acquaintance. (*Drinks.*)

MARLOWE: (*To HASTINGS.*) Just what the fellow at the inn said. But he's a character, and I'll humor him a little. Sir, my service to you. (*Drinks.*) From the excellence of your cup I suppose you have a good deal of trade in this part of the country. Especially during elections.

HARDCASTLE: No, sir, I have long given that work over. Since our betters have hit upon the expedient of electing each other.

HARDCASTLE: So, then, you have no turn for politics?

HARDCASTLE: Not in the least. There was a time I fretted myself about the mistakes of government, like other people; but finding myself every day growing more angry, and the government growing no better, I left it to mend itself.

HASTINGS: So what with eating up stairs, and drinking below, receiving your friends within, and amusing them without, you lead a good pleasant bustling life of it.

HARDCASTLE: I do stir about a great deal, that's certain. Half the differences of the parish are settled in this very parlor.

MARLOWE: I must say your cup is quite good, old gentleman, better than any in Westminster-hall.

HARDCASTLE: Yes, and I add to my cup a little of my philosophy.

MARLOWE: Philosophy?

HASTINGS: So then, if you find your guests reasonable, you attack the problem with your philosophy; but if you find they have no reason, you attack them with this. Here's your health, my philosopher. (*Drinks.*)

HARDCASTLE: Very good; ha! ha! You know, you put me in mind of Prince Eugene, when he fought the Turks at the battle of Belgrade.

MARLOWE: Instead of the battle of Belgrade, I believe it's almost time to talk about supper. What has your philosophy got in the house for supper?

HARDCASTLE: For supper, sir!

MARLOWE: Yes, sir, supper, sir; I begin to feel an appetite. I expect I'll eat quite heartily tonight, I promise you.

HARDCASTLE: Why, really, sir, as for supper I can't actually tell. My Dorothy and the cook-maid settle these things between them. I leave these kind of things entirely to them.

MARLOWE: You do, do you?

HARDCASTLE: Entirely. By the bye, I believe they are in actual consultation upon what's for supper this very moment in the kitchen.

MARLOWE: Then I hope they'll admit me into their council. When I travel, I always chose to regulate my own supper. Let the cook be called. No offense I hope, sir.

HARDCASTLE: O no, sir, none in the least; but Bridget, the cook-maid, is not very open to suggestion about such things. If we send for her, she might scold us all out of the house.

HASTINGS: Let's see what you have on your menu then. I always match my appetite to the bill of fare.

MARLOWE: Yes, I think I should like to see the menu as well.

HARDCASTLE: Of course, sir. Roger, bring us the "menu" for to-night's supper (*ROGER exits*): I believe it's ready—Your manner, Mr. Hastings, puts me in mind of my uncle, Colonel Wallop. It was a saying of his, that no man was sure of his supper till he had eaten it.

Hastings: (*To MARLOWE.*) His uncle a colonel! We'll soon hear of his mother being a justice of the peace.

MARLOWE: (*Perusing.*) What is this? The first course; the second course; the dessert? Far too much. Two or three little things, clean and comfortable, will do.

HASTINGS: But let's hear it.

MARLOWE: (*Reading.*) For the first course, a pig and prune sauce.

HASTINGS: A pig?

Marlowe: And prune sauce.

BOTH: No, no. That will not do.

HARDCASTLE: But, gentlemen, to men that are hungry, pig with prune sauce is very good eating.

Marlowe: Second, a calf's tongue and brains.

HASTINGS: Let's not have the brains, my good sir, I don't like them.

MARLOWE: You could put them on a plate by themselves. I do.

HARDCASTLE: Gentlemen, you are my guests, make what alterations you please. Is there anything else?

MARLOWE: Item, a pork pie, a boiled rabbit and sausages, a Florentine, a shaking pudding, and a dish of tiff—taff—taffety cream.

HASTINGS: What is all of this? This cost as much as dinner at the French ambassador's table. I'm for plain eating.

HARDCASTLE: I'm sorry, gentlemen, that I have nothing you like, but if there be anything you have a particular fancy to…

MARLOWE: Actually, just send us what you please. So much for supper. And now to see that our beds are aired, and properly taken care of.

HARDCASTLE: Leave that to me. You shall not stir a step.

MARLOWE: Leave that to you! I protest, sir, I always look to these things myself.

HARDCASTLE: I must insist, sir, you'll make yourself easy on that count.

MARLOWE: You see I'm resolved to do it.

Hardcastle: Well, sir, I'm resolved at least to attend you. (*Exit MARLOWE and HARDCASTLE.*)

HASTINGS: (*Alone.*) This fellow's civilities begin to grow troublesome. (*Enter CONSTANCE.*) Constance, by all that's happy!

CONSTANCE: My dear Hastings! Why didn't you let me know you were coming?

HASTINGS: Coming? I could never have hoped to meet my dearest Constance at an inn.

CONSTANCE: An inn! surely you mistake: my aunt, my guardian, lives here. What could make you to think this house is an inn?

HASTINGS: My friend, Mr. Marlowe, and I have been

sent here under the impression that this an inn. A young fellow, whom we accidentally met at a pub, directed us here.

CONSTANCE: That must be one of my cousin's tricks. You've have often heard me talk of him. (*Laughing.*)

HASTINGS: The one your aunt intends for you? That's who I was worried about?

CONSTANCE: You have nothing to fear from him, I assure you. You'd adore him, if you knew how heartily he despises me. My aunt knows it too, and has decided to court me for him. She actually begins to think she has made a conquest.

HASTINGS: Constance, I jumped at this opportunity of my friend's visit here to get admittance into the family. The horses are now fatigued with their journey, but they'll soon be refreshed; and then, if you will trust me, we shall soon be landed in France, where the laws of marriage are respected.

CONSTANCE: My dear Hastings, I am ready to marry you, yet I should leave my little fortune behind with reluctance. It was left to me by my uncle and chiefly consists in jewels. I have been persuading my aunt to let me wear them. I believe I'm very near succeeding. The instant they are put into my possession, you shall find me ready to make them and myself yours.

HASTINGS: Forget the jewels. You are all I desire. In the mean time, my friend Marlowe must not be let into his mistake. His reserve and manner is such, that if he were informed of it, he would instantly leave the house before we could do anything.

CONSTANCE: I have an idea. This way…(*They confer. Enter MARLOWE.*)

MARLOWE: These people are more than I can bear. My host seems to think it ill manners to leave me alone, so he and his old-fashioned wife are both trying to be my shadow. They talk of coming to sup with us! —What have we got here?

HASTINGS: My dear Charles! The most fortunate accident! Who do you think has just arrived?

MARLOWE: I cannot guess.

HASTINGS: Our mistresses! Allow me to introduce Miss Constance Neville. She and Miss Hardcastle were dining in the neighborhood and they called here on their return to take fresh horses. Miss Hardcastle has just stepped into the next room, and will be back in an instant. Wasn't it the most fortunate thing in the world?

MARLOWE: Oh! yes. Very fortunate—a most joyful encounter—George, I think we should postpone the happiness till tomorrow?—Tomorrow at her own house—It will be every bit as convenient—and rather more respectful. Tomorrow let it be.

CONSTANCE: By no means, sir. She knows you are in the house, and insist on seeing you.

Marlowe: O! the devil! Hem! Hem! Hastings, you must not go. You are to assist me, you know. I shall be confoundedly ridiculous. Yet, hang it! I'll take courage.

HASTINGS: Pshaw, man! Once you start it'll all be good. She's only a woman, you know.

MARLOWE: And, of all women, the one I dread most to encounter.

(*Enter KATE, as returned from walking, a bonnet, etc.*)

HASTINGS: It is my pleasure to introduce you two; Miss Hardcastle, Mr. Marlowe. I'm sure upon making acquaintance you will find that you are well met.

KATE: (*After a pause, in which he appears very uneasy and disconcerted.*) I'm glad of your safe arrival, sir. I'm told you had some accidents by the way.

MARLOWE: Only a few, ma...ma...mmmma...madam. Yes, we had some. Yes, madam, a good many accidents, but should be be be sorry—ma...madam—or rather glad of any ack...ack...ack...accidents—that are so agreeably con... concluded. Hem!

HASTINGS: (*To him.*) You never spoke better in your whole life. Keep it up.

KATE: I'm afraid you flatter, sir. You who have seen so much of the world can surely find little entertainment in an obscure corner of the country.

MARLOWE: (*Gathering courage.*) I have in...in...in...in... indeed lived in the world, ma...madam; but I have kept very little com...com...company. I have been but an ob...ob... ob...observer of life, madam, while others were enjoying it.

CONSTANCE: But that, I am told, is the way to enjoy it the best.

HASTINGS: (*To him.*) Once more, into the breach, dear friend.

MARLOWE: (*To him.*) Stand by me, and when I'm down, throw in a word or two, to set me up again.

KATE: I fear, you must have had much more to censure than to approve. (Long pause during which Marlowe is speechless.)

HASTINGS: Well, Miss Hardcastle, I see that you and Mr. Marlowe are going to be very good company. I believe there is no need for us to be here.

MARLOWE: No! Mr. Hastings, we like your company. (*To him.*) George, you can't leave us.

HASTINGS: Our presence will only spoil the conversation, so we'll retire to the next room. (*Exit*)

KATE: (*After a pause.*) Surely you have not always been an observer. The ladies, I imagine, have employed some part of your time.

MARLOWE: (*Relapsing into timidity.*) Pardon me, madam, I—I—I—so far have only read read read—only—how to— deserve them.

KATE: Some say that is the very worst way to gain them.

MARLOWE: Perhaps so, madam. But I…only em…em… employ serious con…con…con…conversation. I… I'm afraid… I am certainly boring you.

KATE: Not at all, sir; there is nothing I like so much as serious conversation myself; I could hear it forever. Indeed, I have often been surprised how a thinking man could ever admire those light topics, where nothing reaches the heart.

MARLOWE: It's—a de…de…dis…disease—of the mind, madam. There are some people who, while actually wanting a—for—um—a—um.

KATE: I understand you, sir. There must be some, who, actually want refined conversation, but pretend to despise it because they are incapable of understanding.

MARLOWE: My my meaning, yes madam, but infinitely better expressed. And I can't help observing—a—a—a—

KATE: You were going to observe, sir——

MARLOWE: I was observing, madam—I I pro…protest, madam, I forget what I was going to observe.

KATE: As do I.

MARLOWE: What?

KATE: Nothing. You were observing, sir, that in this age of hypocrisy—something about hypocrisy, sir.

MARLOWE: Yes, madam. In this age of hypocrisy there are few who upon close inspection do not—a—a—a—

KATE: I understand you perfectly, sir.

MARLOWE: Really?

KATE: You mean that in this hypocritical age many condemn in public what they practice in private. Furthermore they think that praising a virtue is the same as possessing it.

MARLOWE: True, ma…ma…madam; those who ta…ta… talk the most virtue tend to have the least of it. But I'm sure I tire you, madam.

KATE: Not in the least, sir; there's something so agreeable and spirited in your manner, such life and force—pray, sir, go on.

MARLOWE: (Pause.) Yes, yes, madam. I was saying——that there are some occasions, when a total want of courage destroys all the—and puts us—upon a—a—a—

KATE: I agree with you entirely; a want of courage upon some occasions makes us look ignorant, and betrays us when we most want to excel.

MARLOWE: Yes, madam. Morally speaking, madam—But I believe Miss Neville is expecting us in the next room.

KATE: Sir, I never was more agreeably entertained in all my life. Pray go on.

MARLOWE: Yes, madam, I was——I'm sure she beckons us to join her. Madam, I'll just go and check for us.

KATE: Well, then, I'll follow.

(*MARLOWE exits.*)

KATE: (*Laughing.*) Was there ever such a disastrous interview? I'm certain he never once looked in my face the whole time. Still, but for his unaccountable bashfulness, I think he'll do nicely. If I could teach him a little confidence, it would be doing somebody a piece of good service. But who is that somebody?—Me, or someone else? (*Exit.*)

(*Enter TONY and CONSTANCE, followed by DOROTHY and HASTINGS*)

TONY: What do you follow me for, cousin Con? I wonder you're not ashamed to be so forward.

Constance: I hope, cousin, I may speak to my own relations.

TONY: Ah, but I know what sort of a relation you want to make me and it won't do. I tell you, cousin Con, it won't do; so keep your distance, I want no nearer relationship. (*She follows, coquetting him.*)

DOROTHY: Well! I vow, Mr. Hastings, you are very entertaining. There's nothing in the world I love to talk of so much as London, and the fashions, though I was never there myself.

HASTINGS: Never there! You amaze me! From your air and manner, I concluded you had been bred there.

DOROTHY: O! sir, you flatter me. We country persons can have no manners at all. I'm in love with the town, and that serves to raise me above some of our rustic neighbors. Who can have manners, that has never seen the Pantheon, and such places where the nobility chiefly resort? All I can do is to enjoy London at second-hand. I do take care to know the latest from the Scandalous Magazine. And I keep up with all the fashions. Pray how do you like my hair, Mr. Hastings?

HASTINGS: Extremely elegant. It is French, I suppose?

DOROTHY: French! No, I dressed it myself from a print in the Ladies' Memorandum-book.

HASTINGS: Indeed! Such a style would turn many a head at a London Ball.

DOROTHY: I believe that one must dress a little particular, or one may get lost in the crowd.

HASTINGS: But that can never be your case, madam. (Bowing.)

DOROTHY: Yet, even though I dress in style it comes to nothing when I have such an old fuddy duddy by my side as Mr. Hardcastle. I can never get him to update any of his clothes. I have often wanted him to cover where he was bald by combing his hair forward, but he claims that looks foolish.

HASTINGS: You are right, madam. Men should do everything in their power to avoid looking old.

DOROTHY: Pray, Mr. Hastings, what do you take to be the most fashionable age about town?

HASTINGS: Some time ago, forty was all the rage; but I'm told the ladies intend to bring up fifty for the coming winter.

DOROTHY: Seriously. Then I shall be too young for the fashion.

HASTINGS: No lady begins now to put on jewels till she's past forty. For instance, Miss there, in a polite circle, would be considered as a pretending child wearing jewels.

DOROTHY: And yet my niece thinks of herself as a woman. She is as fond of jewels, as the oldest of us all.

HASTINGS: Your niece, is she? And that young gentleman, a brother of yours, I should presume?

DOROTHY: My son, sir. They are engaged to each other. Observe their little sports. They fall in and out ten times a day, as if they were man and wife already. (*To them.*) Well, Tony, child, what soft things are you saying to your cousin Constance this evening?

TONY: I have been saying no soft things. I'm telling her to stop following me! I've no place in the house now to myself, but the stable.

DOROTHY: Never mind him, Con, my dear. He tells a different story behind your back.

CONSTANCE: I know. He pretends in public so he can be forgiven in private.

TONY: That's a confounded—crack.

DOROTHY: Ah! he's a sly one. Don't you think they look a bit alike, Mr. Hastings? They're near of size, too. Back to back, my pretties, let Mr. Hastings see you. Come, Tony.

CONSTANCE: Oh, he has almost cracked my head.

DOROTHY: For shame, Tony. You a man, and behave so!

TONY: If I'm a man, let me have my fortune. I'll not be made a fool of no longer.

DOROTHY: Is this all that I'm to get for the pains I have

taken in your education? I rocked you in your cradle, and fed that pretty mouth with a spoon!

Tony: I tell you, I'll not be made a fool of no longer.

Dorothy: Wasn't it all for your good? Wasn't it all for your good?

Tony: I wish you'd let me and my good alone. If I'm to have any good, let it come by itself without you needing to hand deliver it.

Dorothy: See he wants to break my heart. He is so thoughtless.

Hastings: Dear madam, permit me to lecture the young gentleman a little. I'm certain I can persuade him to his duty.

Dorothy: Well, I must retire. Come, Constance, my love. You see, Mr. Hastings, the wretchedness of my situation: was ever a woman so plagued with a dear sweet, pretty, provoking, undutiful boy? (*Exeunt DOROTHY and CONSTANCE.*)

Tony: Don't mind her. Let her cry. She enjoys it. I have seen her and sister cry over a book for an hour together; and they said they liked the book better because it made them cry.

Hastings: Then you're no friend to the ladies, I find?

Tony: I only say what I see.

Hastings: Apparently you don't seem to care for the one of your mother's choosing? And yet she appears to me a pretty well-tempered girl.

Tony: That's because you don't know her as well as I. Egad! I know every inch about her; and there's not a more bitter cantankerous toad in all Christendom. I have seen her since the height of that. She has as many tricks as a hare in a thicket.

Hastings: To me she appears sensible and silent.

Tony: Sure, before company. But when she's with her friends, she's as loud as a hog in a gate.

HASTINGS: But there is a meek modesty about her that charms me.

TONY: Yes, but cross her just a little and she kicks up, and you're flung in a ditch.

HASTINGS: But you must agree she is actually quite pretty. Yes, you must allow her some beauty.

TONY: Bandbox! She's all a made-up thing, man. Ah! could you but see Bet Bouncer of these parts, you might then talk of beauty. She has two eyes as black as sloes, and cheeks as broad and red as a pulpit cushion. She'd make two of that one.

HASTINGS: Well, what would you say to a friend that would take "that one" off your hands?

TONY: Go on?

HASTINGS: Would you thank him that would take Miss Neville, and leave you to happiness and your dear Betsy?

TONY: Of course, but where is there such a friend. Who would take her?

HASTINGS: I would be willing. If you will assist me, I'll whisk her off to France, and you shall never hear more of her.

TONY: Assist you! Egad, I will to the last drop of my blood. I'll even clap a pair of horses to your carriage that shall trundle you off in a twinkling, and even get you a part of her fortune beside, in jewels. Perhaps that will help you not change your mind.

HASTINGS: My dear squire, we have a deal.

TONY: Come along, then, let's not waste any time. (*Singing,*) *When papa papered the parlor you couldn't see pa for paste.*

Scene 4

The House

HARDCASTLE: What could Sir Charles mean by saying

his son is the most modest young man in town? He appears the most impudent piece of brass that ever spoke with a tongue. He has taken possession of my easy chair by the fire-side. He took off his boots in the parlor, and told me to see them taken care of. I wonder how my Kate is taking his impudence. She will certainly be shocked at it.

(Enter KATE, plainly dressed.)

HARDCASTLE: Well, Kate, I see you have changed your dress, as I instructed you; and yet, apparently there was no good reason to do so. This "modest" gentleman I spoke of has turned out to be anything but.

KATE: You taught me to expect something extraordinary, and that is exactly what I found.

HARDCASTLE: I was never so surprised in my life!

KATE: I never saw anything like it: and he is a man of the world too!

HARDCASTLE: Exactly, he learned it all abroad—what a fool I was, to think a young man could learn modesty by traveling.

KATE: He seems to come by it naturally.

HARDCASTLE: I suspect it was a good deal assisted by bad company, especially in France.

KATE: Surely not, papa. The French could never have taught him to be so timid, so awkward, so bashful in his manner.

HARDCASTLE: What are you talking about, child?

KATE: Mr. Marlowe. His timidity struck me at the first sight.

HARDCASTLE: Then your first sight deceived you. I think him one of the most brazen first sights that ever astonished my senses.

KATE: You must be teasing me. I never saw anyone so modest.

HARDCASTLE: It's you who are teasing me. I never saw such a bouncing, swaggering puppy since I was born.

KATE: That's surprising! He met me with a respectful bow, a stammering voice, and a reluctance to look one in the face.

HARDCASTLE: He met me with a loud voice, a lordly air, and a familiarity that made my blood freeze.

KATE: He treated me with diffidence and respect.

HARDCASTLE: He spoke to me as if he knew me all his life. He asked twenty questions, and never waited for an answer. He interrupted my best remarks and when I was in my best story of the Duke of Marlborough he asked me for a glass of punch.

KATE: Punch?

HARDCASTLE: Yes, Kate, he asked your father if he was a maker of punch!

KATE: One of us must certainly be mistaken.

HARDCASTLE: From what I've seen so far he shall never have my consent.

KATE: If he be the sullen thing I've seen, he shall never have mine.

HARDCASTLE: Then we are agreed—to reject him.

KATE: Yes: but upon conditions. For if you should find him less impertinent, and I more presuming... if you find him more respectful, and I more forward... I don't know... he's actually... What I mean is, we don't meet that many men here in the country

HARDCASTLE: The first appearance has finished me. I'm seldom deceived by first impressions.

Kate: Yet there may be many good qualities under that first appearance.

HARDCASTLE: When a girl finds a fellow's outside to her taste, she then sets about guessing the rest of his furniture. A handsome face stands for good sense and every virtue.

KATE: I hope, sir, a conversation begun with a compliment to my good sense, won't end with a sneer at my understanding?

HARDCASTLE: Pardon me, Kate. But if young Mr. Brazen can find the art of reconciling contradictions, there may still be some hope.

KATE: Since one of us must be mistaken we should investigate further.

HARDCASTLE: Agreed. But depend on't I'm in the right.

KATE: And depend on't I'm not much in the wrong. (*Both exit.*)

(*Enter TONY, running in with a box.*)

TONY: I have got them. Here they are. My cousin Con's necklaces, bobs and all. My mother shan't cheat the poor souls out of her fortune.

(*Enter HASTINGS.*)

HASTINGS: My dear friend, how has it gone with your mother? Have you at last convinced her that you love your cousin? Our horses will be refreshed in a short time, and we shall soon be ready to set off.

TONY: Never fear! And here's something of a going away present (*giving the box*); your sweetheart's jewels. Keep them: and hang those that would rob you of one of them.

HASTINGS: But how did you get them from your mother?

TONY: Ask me no questions, and I'll tell you no lies. If I didn't have the keys to every drawer in mother's bureau, how could I go to the alehouse so often as I do? I say, an honest man may rob himself of what is already his.

HASTINGS: Thousands do it every day. But to be plain

with you; Miss Neville is endeavoring to procure these from her aunt this very instant. If she succeeds, that will be the best way of obtaining them.

TONY: Well, keep them, till you know how it will be. I know how it will be well enough; she'd as soon part with the only sound tooth in her head as give up those jewels.

HASTINGS: But I dread her resentment, when she finds she has lost them.

TONY: Pish! Never you mind her resentment, leave *me* to manage that. I don't value her resentment the bounce of a cracker. Zounds! here they are. Go!

(Exit HASTINGS. Enter DOROTHY and CONSTANCE.)

DOROTHY: Constance, you amaze me. Such a girl as you wanting jewels! There will be time enough for jewels, my dear, when you age and your beauty begins to fade somewhat.

CONSTANCE: But what will repair beauty at forty, will certainly improve it at twenty, madam.

DOROTHY: Yours, my dear, needs no assistance. That natural blush is beyond a thousand ornaments. Besides, child, jewels are quite out of fashion at present.

CONSTANCE: Who knows, madam, but that somebody who shall remain nameless might like me best with all my little finery about me?

DOROTHY: Just look in the mirror. What do you think, Tony, my dear? Does your cousin Con need any jewels in your eyes to set off her beauty?

TONY: Well, she may someday.

CONSTANCE: My dear aunt, if you knew how it would oblige me.

DOROTHY: A box of old-fashioned jewels would make you look so out of fashion. Besides, I'm not really certain I can find them. They may be missing, for all I know.

Tony: (*Apart to DOROTHY.*) Then why don't you tell her so at once, since she wants them so much? Tell her they're lost. It's the only way to quiet her. Say they're lost, and I'll be your witness.

Dorothy: (*Apart to TONY.*) You know, my dear, I'm only keeping them for you. So if I say they're gone, and you bear me witness, that should work. He! he! he!

Tony: Egad! I'll say I saw them taken out with my own eyes.

Constance: I only want them for a day, madam. Just to be permitted to show them as relics, and then they may be locked up again.

Dorothy: To be plain with you, my dear Constance, if I could find them you should have them this instant. They're missing, I assure you. Lost, for all I know

Constance: I don't believe it! This is a shallow pretense to deny me. I know they are too valuable to be so slightly kept.

Dorothy: Don't be alarmed, Constance. If they are lost, I know I must restore an equivalent value. But my son knows they are missing, and not to be found.

Tony: To that I can bear witness. They are missing, and not to be found; I'll take my oath on it.

Dorothy: You must learn patience, my dear. Though we lose our fortune, yet we should not lose our patience. See me, how calm I am.

Constance: People are generally calm at the misfortunes of others.

Dorothy: I wonder that a girl of your good sense should waste a thought about such trinkets. We shall soon find them; and in the mean time you can use my garnets till your rubies are found.

Constance: I detest garnets.

DOROTHY: They are the best things in the world to set off a clear complexion. You have often seen how well they look upon me. You *shall* have them. (*Exit.*)

CONSTANCE: Was ever anything so provoking as to mislay my own jewels, and force me to wear her ugly garnets?

TONY: Don't be a fool. If she gives you the garnets take what you can get. The jewels are already yours. I have stolen them out of her bureau, and she does not know it. Fly to your Hastings, he'll tell you more of the matter. Leave me to manage her.

CONSTANCE: My dear cousin!

TONY: Vanish. She's here, and has missed them already. (*Exit CONSTANCE. Enter DOROTHY.*)

DOROTHY: Thieves! Robbers! We are cheated, plundered, broke open, undone.

TONY: What's the matter, what's the matter, mamma? I hope nothing has happened to any of the good family!

DOROTHY: We are robbed. My bureau has been broken open, the jewels taken out, and I'm undone.

TONY: Oh! Is that all? Ha! ha! ha! Bravo, I never saw it acted better in my life. Egad, I thought you was ruined in earnest, ha! ha! ha!

DOROTHY: Why, boy, I *am* ruined in earnest. My bureau has been broken open, and all taken away.

TONY: Stick to that: ha! ha! ha! Stick to that. I'll bear witness, you know; call me to bear witness.

DOROTHY: I tell you, Tony, by all that's precious, the jewels are gone, and I shall be ruined for ever.

TONY: Sure I know they're gone, and I'm to say so.

DOROTHY: My dearest Tony, hear me! They're gone, I say.

TONY: Mamma, you make me laugh, ha! ha! I know who took them well enough, ha! ha! ha!

DOROTHY: Was there ever such a blockhead, that you

can't tell the difference between jest and earnest? I tell you I'm not in jest.

TONY: That's right, that's right; you must be in a bitter passion, and then nobody will suspect either of us. I'll bear witness that they are gone.

DOROTHY: Was there ever such a ninny, that won't hear me? Can you bear witness that you're no better than a fool? Was there ever a poor woman so beset with fools on one hand, and thieves on the other?

TONY: I can bear witness to that.

DOROTHY: Bear witness again, you blockhead you, and I'll run you out of the room. My poor niece, what will become of her? And you laughing as if you enjoyed my distress?

TONY: I can bear witness to that.

DOROTHY: Do you insult me, monster? I'll teach you to vex your mother.

TONY: I can bear witness to that. (*He runs off, she follows him.*)

(*Enter KATE and BRIDGET.*)

KATE: What an unaccountable creature is that brother of mine, to send them to the house pretending it was an inn! ha! ha! There are few can match Tony's brass.

BRIDGET: What is more, madam, the young gentleman, as we just passed by, saw your present dress and asked me if you were the barmaid. He mistook you for the barmaid, madam.

KATE: Did he? Then as I live, I'm resolved to keep up the delusion. Tell me, how do you like my present dress?

BRIDGET: It's the dress, madam, that every lady wears in the country.

KATE: And are you sure he does not remember my face?

BRIDGET: Certain of it.

KATE: I thought as much. We spoke for some time together, but his fears were such, that he never once looked at me during the interview.

BRIDGET: But what do you hope to gain by keeping him in his mistake?

KATE: In the first place I shall be seen. Then I shall perhaps make an acquaintance. But my chief aim is, to take my gentleman off his guard and see what this Mr. Marlowe is really like. You had better go.

(Exit BRIDGET. Enter MARLOWE.)

MARLOWE: What a racquet in every part of the house! I scarce have a moment's rest. If I go to the best room, there I find my host telling his made up stories. If I fly to the gallery, there we have my hostess with her curtsey down to the ground.

KATE: Did ya call, sir? Did your honor call?

Marlowe: (*Musing*) As for Miss Hardcastle, she's too grave and sentimental for me.

KATE: Did your honor call? (*She places herself before him, he turning away.*)

MARLOWE: No, child. (*Musing.*) Besides, from the glimpse I had of her, I think she squints.

KATE: I'm sure, sir, I 'erd the bell ring.

MARLOWE: No, no. (*Musing.*) I have pleased my father by coming down, and tomorrow I'll please myself by returning.

KATE: Perhaps the other gentleman called, sir?

MARLOWE: I tell you, no.

KATE: But I 'erd the bell, sir!

MARLOWE: No, no, I tell you. (*Looks full in her face.*) Yes, child, I think I did call. I wanted—I wanted—I vow, child, you are vastly handsome.

KATE: Oh, sir, you'll make one ashamed.

MARLOWE: I never saw a more sprightly malicious eye. Yes, yes, my dear, I did call. Have you got any of your—a—what do you call it in the house?

KATE: No, sir, we have been out of that for ten days.

MARLOWE: I find one may call in this house to very little purpose. Suppose I should call for a taste, just by way of a trial, of the nectar of your lips; would I be disappointed in that request too.

KATE: Nectar! Nectar! That's a liquor there's no call for that in these parts. French, I suppose. We sell no French wines here, sir.

MARLOWE: I'm interested in true English growth, I assure you.

KATE: Then it's odd I should not know it. We brew all sorts of wines in this house, and I have lived here these eighteen years.

MARLOWE: Eighteen years! Really? How old are you?

KATE: O! sir, I must not tell my age.

MARLOWE: To guess at this distance, you can't be much above thirty (*approaching*). Yet, nearer, I don't think so much (*approaching*). By coming close to some women they look younger still; but when we come very close indeed—(*attempting to kiss her*).

KATE: Pray, sir, keep your distance. One would think you wanted to know one's age, as they do horses, by looking in the mouth.

MARLOWE: If you keep me at this distance, how is it possible you and I can ever be acquainted?

KATE: And who wants to be acquainted with you? I want no such acquaintance. I'm sure you didn't treat Miss Hardcastle, that was here awhile ago, in this manner. I'll warrant, before her you kept bowing to the ground, and talked as if you was before a justice of peace.

MARLOWE: I in awe of her, child? Ha! ha! ha! A mere awkward squinting thing; no, no. I find you don't know me. I laughed and rallied her a little; but I let her off easy.

KATE: O! then, sir, you are a favorite among the ladies?

MARLOWE: Yes, my dear, a great favorite. At the Ladies' Club in town I'm called their agreeable Rattle. Rattle, child, is not my real name, but one I'm known by.

KATE: Then it must be a very merry place, I suppose?

MARLOWE: Yes, as merry as cards, supper, wine, and women can make. Do you do any other work here, child?

KATE: For sure. There's not a screen or quilt in the whole house but what can bear witness to that.

MARLOWE: Then you must show me your embroidery. If you want a judge of your work, you must allow me. (*Seizing her hand.*)

KATE: Yes, well, the colors do not look well by candlelight. You shall see all in the morning. (*Struggling.*)

MARLOWE: And why not now, my angel? Drat, the old host is coming! Just my luck.

(*Exit MARLOWE. Enter HARDCASTLE, who stands in surprise.*)

HARDCASTLE: So, madam, I find this is your "modest" lover? This is your "humble" admirer, who is reluctant to look one in the face? Kate, you should be ashamed to deceive your father so.

KATE: Trust me, dear papa, he's still the modest man I first took him for; you'll be convinced of it as well as I.

HARDCASTLE: I'm convinced his impudence is infectious! Didn't I see him seize your hand? Didn't I see him haul you about like a barmaid? And now you talk of his respect and his modesty?

KATE: If I can convince you of his modesty I hope you'll forgive both he and me.

HARDCASTLE: Do you take me for a simpleton? I tell you, I'll not be convinced. I am convinced. He has scarce been three hours in the house, and he has already encroached on all my prerogatives. You may like his impudence, and call it modesty; but my son-in-law, madam, must have very different qualifications.

KATE: Just give me this night to convince you.

HARDCASTLE: I am thinking to turn him out this very hour.

KATE: Give me that hour then.

HARDCASTLE: One hour. But no trifling. All fair and open, do you mind me.

KATE: Thank you, father. Only one more hour and we can wrap up this whole affair.

Curtain

ACT II
Scene 1

The House. Enter HASTINGS and CONSTANCE

HASTINGS: Are you sure; Sir Charles Marlowe is expected here this night!

CONSTANCE: I saw his letter to Mr. Hardcastle, in which he tells him he intends setting out a few hours after his son.

HASTINGS: Then we must complete all before he arrives. He knows me. My name, and perhaps my purpose, will be known to the rest of the family.

CONSTANCE: The jewels, I hope, are safe?

HASTINGS: Yes, I have sent them to Marlowe, who keeps the keys of our baggage. In the mean time, I'll go to prepare matters for our elopement. The squire has promised a fresh pair of horses. (*Exit.*)

CONSTANCE: I'll go and amuse my aunt with the pretense of a violent passion for my cousin. (*Exit. Enter MARLOWE, followed by ROGER.*)

MARLOWE: I wonder what Hastings could mean by sending me so valuable a thing to keep for him. Have you deposited the casket with the landlady, as I ordered you? You put it into her own hands?

ROGER: Yes, your honor.

MARLOWE: She said she'd keep it safe?

ROGER: Yes, she said she'd keep it safe enough. She asked me how I came by it; and said she had a great mind to make me give an account of myself. (*Exit ROGER.*)

MARLOWE: At least the box is safe. What a strange people inhabit this house. But I can't stop thinking about this little barmaid.

(Enter HASTINGS.)

HASTINGS: Bless me! I quite forgot to tell her that I intended we should meet at the bottom of the garden. Ah, Marlowe, there you are and in good spirits too!

MARLOWE: Congratulate me, George! I may be modest but I don't lack for success among the women.

Hastings: Some women, you mean. What success have you had lately?

MARLOWE: Did you see the tempting, lovely little thing, that runs about the house jangling a bunch of keys?

HASTINGS: Perhaps, I have?

MARLOWE: She's mine, you rogue you. Such fire, such motion, such eyes, such lips.

HASTINGS: Are you so very sure of her?

MARLOWE: She talked of showing me her work up stairs, and I am to improve the pattern.

HASTINGS: Charles, how can you go about to rob a woman of her honor?

MARLOWE: Pshaw! We all know the honor of the barmaid of an inn. I don't intend to rob her, take my word for it; there's nothing in this house I won't honestly pay for.

HASTINGS: I believe the girl has virtue.

MARLOWE: And if she has, I should be the last man in the world that would attempt to corrupt it.

HASTINGS: You have taken care, I hope, of the box I sent you to lock up?

MARLOWE: Yes, yes. It's safe enough. I have taken care of it. I have taken better precautions for you than you did for yourself.

HASTINGS: What do you mean?

MARLOWE: I have sent it to the landlady for safe keeping.

HASTINGS: To the landlady!

MARLOWE: The landlady.

HASTINGS: You did?

MARLOWE: I did. She's to be answerable for it being kept safe.

HASTINGS: She'll keep it safe alright.

MARLOWE: I believe you'll have to agree I acted wisely. You seem a little disconcerted though. Has something happened?

HASTINGS: No, nothing. Never was in better spirits in all my life. And so you left it with the landlady, who, no doubt, very readily took the charge.

MARLOWE: She not only kept the casket, but, she almost kept the messenger too. Ha! ha! ha!

HASTINGS: He! he! he! They're safe, however.

MARLOWE: As a guinea in a miser's purse.

HASTINGS: Well, Charles, I'll leave you to your meditations on the pretty barmaid, and, may you be as successful for yourself, as you have been for me! (*Exit.*)

MARLOWE: Thank you, George: I ask no more.

(*Enter HARDCASTLE.*)

HARDCASTLE: Mr. Marlowe, I'm your very humble servant. (*Bowing low.*)

MARLOWE: Sir, your humble servant.

HARDCASTLE: I believe, sir, that no man alive ought to be more welcome here than your father's son.

MARLOWE: I generally make my father's son welcome wherever he goes.

HARDCASTLE: I believe you do, sir, but though I don't besmirch your own conduct, that of your servants is insufferable. Their manner of drinking is setting a very bad example in this house, I assure you.

MARLOWE: My good sir, that is no fault of mine. If they don't drink as they ought, they are to blame. I ordered them not to spare the cellar. My directions were, that as I did not drink myself, they should undertake to make up for my deficiencies.

HARDCASTLE: Then they had your orders for what they do?

MARLOWE: They had, I assure you.

HARDCASTLE: Sir; I have submitted to your insolence for more than four hours, and I see no likelihood of its coming to an end. I desire that you and your drunken pack may leave my house directly.

MARLOWE: Leave your house! Surely you jest. I'm doing what I can to please you.

HARDCASTLE: I tell you, sir, you don't please me; so I desire you'll leave my house.

MARLOWE: You cannot be serious? At this time of night?

HARDCASTLE: I tell you, sir, I am serious! And now that my passions are roused, I say this house is mine, sir; this house is mine, and I command you to leave it directly.

MARLOWE: Make me. I won't stir a step. This your house? It's my house! This is my house. Mine, while I choose to stay. What right have you to bid me leave this house?

HARDCASTLE: To come to my house, to call for what you like, to turn me out of my own chair, to insult the family, to order your servants to get drunk, and then to tell me, "This house is mine, sir." By all that's impudent, it makes me laugh. Ha! ha! ha! Pray, sir, as you take the house, what about taking the rest of the furniture? There's a pair of silver candlesticks, and there's a fire-screen, and here's a pair of brazen-nosed bellows; perhaps you may take a fancy to them?

MARLOWE: Bring me your bill, sir; bring me your bill, and let's have no more talk.

HARDCASTLE: There are a set of prints, too. Take them for your own apartment?

MARLOWE: Bring me your bill, I say; and I'll leave you and your infernal house directly.

HARDCASTLE: Then there's a mahogany table.

MARLOWE: My bill, I say.

HARDCASTLE: I had forgot the great chair for your own slumbers, after a hearty meal.

MARLOWE: Zounds! bring me my bill, I say, and let's hear no more on't.

HARDCASTLE: From your father's letter to me, I was taught to expect a well-bred modest man, but now I find you are no better than a bully! He will be down here presently, and shall hear about this. (*Exit.*)

MARLOWE: How's this? Have I mistaken the house? Everything looks like an inn. There is even a barmaid, and here she comes. Not so fast, child? A word with you.

(Enter KATE.)

KATE: Let it be short, then. I'm in a hurry.

MARLOWE: Pray, child, answer me one question. What are you, and what is your business in this house?

KATE: A relation of the family, sir.

MARLOWE: What, a poor relation?

KATE: Yes, sir. A poor relation, appointed to keep the keys, and to see that the guests want nothing in my power to give them.

MARLOWE: So, you are the barmaid of this inn?

KATE: Inn! O what brought that in your head? One of the best families in the country keep an inn? Ha! ha! ha! old Mr. Hardcastle's 'ouse an inn!

MARLOWE: Mr. Hardcastle's house! Is this Mr. Hardcastle's house, child?

KATE: Sure! Whose else should it be?

MARLOWE: Oh, oh, oh confound my stupid head, I shall be laughed at all over town. To mistake this house for an inn, and my father's old friend for an innkeeper! Ah, may I be hanged, my dear, but I mistook you for the barmaid.

KATE: Dear me! I'm sure there's nothing in my behavior to put me on a level with a barmaid.

MARLOWE: No, my dear, nothing. I've made such a list of blunders, and you ended up on it. I've seen everything the wrong way. But it's over. I can no more show my face in this house.

KATE: I hope, sir, I'm not to blame. I should be sorry to cause distress to any gentleman who has been so polite, and said so many civil things to me. I'm sure I should be sorry if he left the family upon my account.

MARLOWE: You are the only part of the family I leave with reluctance. Unfortunately, the difference of our stations makes an honorable connexion impossible; and I can never harbor a thought of bringing ruin upon one whose only fault was being too lovely.

KATE: I am sure my family is as good as Miss Hardcastle's; and though I'm poor, that's no great misfortune to one who is content. Until this moment, I never thought that it was bad to be poor.

MARLOWE: Why now? What has changed your mind?

KATE: Because it separates me from... you.

MARLOWE: If I were free to make my own choice, I could so easily fix my choice on you. But I owe too much to the opinion and authority of my father; so that... I can scarcely speak it.... Farewell. (*Exit.*)

KATE: Well! He is a man of merit. He shall not go. I'll

still play this character but will undeceive my papa, who hopefully may laugh and change his mind. (*Exit. Enter TONY and CONSTANCE.*)

TONY: Steal for yourselves the next time. I have done my duty. She has got the jewels again, and that's all there is to it. At least she believes it was all a mistake of the servants.

CONSTANCE: My dear cousin, you can't forsake us in this distress. If she in the least suspects that I am going off, I shall be locked up, or sent to my aunt Pedigree's, which is ten times worse.

TONY: To be sure, aunts of all kinds are desperate bad things. But what can I do? I have got you a pair of horses that will fly like the wind. And I have courted you nicely before her face; and... here she comes, we must court a bit more. (*They retire, and seem to fondle. Enter DOROTHY.*)

DOROTHY: What do I see? Fondling together, as I'm alive. I never saw you so sprightly before, my sweet Tony. I have caught you, my pretty doves? What, exchanging stolen glances and sweet murmurs? Ah!

TONY: As for murmurs, mother, we grumble a little now and then, to be sure. But there's no love lost between us.

DOROTHY: Spats are a mere sprinkling upon the flame of love to make it burn brighter.

CONSTANCE: Cousin Tony promises to give us more of his company at home. Indeed, he shan't leave us any more.

TONY: No, I'd sooner leave my horse in a pound, than leave you when you smile so. Your laugh makes you so becoming.

CONSTANCE: Ah cousin! Who can help but admire that natural humor, that pleasant, broad, thoughtless (*patting his cheek*) bold face.

TONY: I'm sure I always loved cousin Con's hazel eyes, and her pretty long fingers, like twigs on the end of a branch.

DOROTHY: You would charm the birds from the trees. I have never been so happy. The jewels, my dear Con, shall be yours. You shall have them. Isn't he a sweet boy, my dear? You shall be married tomorrow, and we'll put off the rest of his education to a more convenient time.

(Enter DIGGORY.)

DIGGORY: Where's the squire? I have got a letter for your worship.

TONY: Give it to my mamma. She reads all my letters first.

DIGGORY: I had orders to deliver it into your own hands.

TONY: Who does it come from?

DIGGORY: You'll have to ask that o' the letter itself.

TONY: I could wish to know though (*turning the letter, and gazing on it*).

CONSTANCE: (Seeing the handwriting she gasps - *To DOROTHY.*) I have not told you, madam, of my cousin's smart answer just now to Mr. Marlowe. We laughed so hardily. You must know, madam.... This way a little, so he won't hear us. (*They confer.*)

TONY: (Still gazing.) This is as cramped a piece of penmanship as ever I saw in my life. I can read your print hand very well. But here are such curves, and squiggles, and dashes, that one can scarce tell the head from the tail.— "To Anthony Lumpkin, Esquire." It's very odd, I can read the outside of my letters, where my own name is, well enough; but when I come to open it, it's all gibberish. That's unfortunate; for the inside of the letter is always the cream of the correspondence.

DOROTHY: Ha! ha! ha! So my son was too hard for the philosopher?

CONSTANCE: Yes, madam; but you must hear the rest.

You'll hear how he puzzled him again.

DOROTHY: He seems strangely puzzled now himself.

TONY: (*Still gazing.*) There are lines all over the place. The person who wrote this must have been drunk. (*Reading.*) Dear Sir,—ah, dear sir. Then there's an M, and a T, and an S, but whether the next is an R or an izzard, confound me, I cannot tell.

DOROTHY: What's that, my dear? Can I give you any assistance?

CONSTANCE: Pray, aunt, let me read it. Nobody reads a cramp hand better than I. (*Twitching the letter from him.*) Do you know who it is from?

TONY: Can't tell. Maybe from Dick Ginger, the feeder.

CONSTANCE: Why, so it is. (*Pretending to read.*) Dear Squire, hoping that you're in health, as I am at this present. The gentlemen of the Shake-bag club has cut the gentlemen of Goose-green quite out of feather. The odds—um—odd battle—um—long fighting—um—here, here, it's all about cocks and fighting; it's of no consequence; here, put it up, put it up. (*Thrusting the crumpled letter upon him.*)

TONY: But I tell you it's of all the consequence in the world. I would not lose the rest of it for a guinea. Here, mother, you make it out. Of no consequence! (*Giving DOROTHY the letter.*)

DOROTHY: What is this?—(*Reads*) "Dear Squire, I'm now waiting for Miss Neville, with a carriage at the bottom of the garden. I expect you'll assist us with a pair of fresh horses, as you promised. Speed is necessary, as the HAG, your mother, will otherwise suspect us! Yours, Hastings."

CONSTANCE: I hope, madam, you'll suspend your resentment for a few moments, and not think that I had anything to do with such a sinister plan.

DOROTHY: (*Curtseying very low.*) Fine spoken, madam,

you are most miraculously polite and engaging, and quite the very pink of courtesy and circumspection. (*Changing her tone.*) And you, you great ill-fashioned oaf, with scarce sense enough to keep your mouth shut: you were joined against me? I'll defeat all of your plots. As for you, madam, since there is a pair of fresh horses ready, it would be a pity to disappoint them. So, if you please, instead of running away with your spark, prepare, this very moment, to run off with *me*. Your aunt Pedigree will keep you secure. You, sir, may mount your horse, and guard us upon the way. (*Exit*)

CONSTANCE: So now I'm completely ruined.

TONY: That's for sure.

CONSTANCE: I should have known better that to get connected with such a stupid fool. After all the nods and signs I made you.

TONY: It was your own cleverness, and not my stupidity, that did you in. You were so sincere with your Shakebags and Goose-greens, that I thought you could never be making believe.

(Enter HASTINGS.)

HASTINGS: So, I find by my servant, that you have shown my letter, and betrayed us.

TONY: It was miss there, who betrayed you. Egad, it was her doing, not mine.

(Enter MARLOWE.)

MARLOWE: So, the joke has been on me has it? I've been rendered contemptible, despised, insulted, laughed at.

CONSTANCE: And there, sir, is the gentleman who caused all of this confusion and trouble.

MARLOWE: Yes, but he's a mere boy and idiot, whose

ignorance and age protect him.

HASTINGS: A poor contemptible booby.

CONSTANCE: That may be true but he had enough cunning and malice to make himself merry with all our embarrassments.

HASTINGS: An insensible cub.

MARLOWE: Full of mischief.

TONY: Stand back! I'll fight you both, one after the other… with… with baskets!

MARLOWE: As for him, he's below resentment. But your conduct, Mr. Hastings, requires an explanation. You knew of my mistakes, yet did not undeceive me.

HASTINGS: As distressed with disappointment as I am now, this is not a time for explanations.

MARLOWE: But, sir…

CONSTANCE: Mr. Marlowe, we didn't know the mistake ourselves till it was too late to undeceive you.

(Enter BRIDGET.)

BRIDGET: My mistress desires you'll get ready immediately, madam. The horses are being hitched. Your hat and things are in the next room. We are to go thirty miles before morning. (*Exit.*)

CONSTANCE: I'll come presently.

MARLOWE: (*To HASTINGS.*) Was it well done, sir, to assist in making me look ridiculous? To expose me to scorn?

HASTINGS: Was it well done, sir, since we are on the subject, to deliver what I entrusted to you, to the care of another?

CONSTANCE: Mr. Hastings! Mr. Marlow! You're only making things worse by this arguing. I implore you…

(Enter BRIDGET.)

BRIDGET: Your cloak, madam. My mistress is impatient.

(*Exit.*)

CONSTANCE: I'm coming. Be patient.

(*Enter BRIDGET.*)

BRIDGET: Your fan, muff, and gloves, madam. The horses are waiting.

CONSTANCE: Mr. Marlowe, if you knew the fate that lies before me, I'm sure it would convert your resentment into pity.

MARLOWE: I'm so distracted with so many passions, that I don't know what I do. Forgive me, madam. George, forgive me. You know my hasty temper.

HASTINGS: Forgive me. The torture of my situation is my only excuse.

CONSTANCE: My dear Hastings, if you care for me as I think you do, as I care for you, then waiting these next three years will only increase the happiness of our future connexion. If...

DOROTHY: (*Within.*) Miss Neville. Constance, why Constance, I say.

CONSTANCE: I'm coming. Constancy, remember, constancy is the word. (*Exit.*)

HASTINGS: How can I stand this? To be so near happiness!

MARLOWE: (*To TONY.*) You see now the effects of your folly. What might be amusement to you, is to others disappointment, and even distress.

TONY: (*From a reverie.*) Egad, I have hit on it! Gentlemen, never fear. Meet me in two hours at the bottom of the garden; and if you don't find Tony Lumpkin a more good-natured fellow than you thought, I'll give you leave to take my best horse, and Bet Bouncer into the bargain.

Scene 2

Later in the House. Enter HASTINGS and ROGER.

HASTINGS: You saw the old lady and Miss Neville drive off, you say?
ROGER: Yes, your honor. They went off in a coach, and the young squire went on horseback. They're thirty miles off by this time.
HASTINGS: Then all my hopes are over.
ROGER: Yes, sir. And Old Sir Charles has arrived. He and the old gentleman of the house have been laughing at Mr. Marlowe's mistake. They are coming this way.
HASTINGS: I must not be seen. Now to my fruitless appointment at the bottom of the garden. It has almost been two hours. (*Exit.*)

(Enter SIR CHARLES and HARDCASTLE.)

HARDCASTLE: Ha! ha! ha! You should have heard him sending forth his commands!
SIR CHARLES: And the way with which I suppose he treated all your protests?
HARDCASTLE: You would think he might have seen something in me above a common innkeeper.
SIR CHARLES: Of course, he mistook you for an uncommon innkeeper, ha! ha! ha!
HARDCASTLE: Well, I'm in too good a spirits to think of anything but joy. My dear friend, this union of our families will make our personal friendships hereditary; and though my daughter's fortune is but small—
SIR CHARLES: There is no need to talk of fortune to me. My son has more than enough already. He only needs a

good virtuous girl to share his happiness and increase it. If they like each other, as you say they do...

HARDCASTLE: If! Man! I tell you they *do* like each other. My daughter as good as told me so.

(Enter MARLOWE.)

MARLOWE: I come, sir, once more, to ask your pardon for my strange conduct. I can scarcely think of my insolence without embarrassment.

HARDCASTLE: Think no more of it; a trifle! An hour or two laughing with my daughter will set all to rights again. She won't hold it against you.

MARLOWE: Sir, I shall always esteem her approval.

HARDCASTLE: "Esteem her approval" is a rather cold phrase, Mr. Marlow; if I am not deceived, you have something more than "esteem" for my daughter?

MARLOWE: Really, sir, I have not really had the happiness of her conversation.

HARDCASTLE: Come, boy, I'm an old fellow, but I know what's what as well as you younger bucks. I know what has passed between you two; but I'll be mum.

MARLOWE: Sir, nothing has passed between us but the most profound respect on my side, and the most distant reserve on hers.

HARDCASTLE: That's not what she says. But she has told no tales, I assure you.

MARLOWE: I never gave her the slightest cause to tell tales.

HARDCASTLE: I like modesty in its place well enough. But this is over-acting, young gentleman. You may be open. Your father and I will like you all the better for it.

MARLOWE: May I die, sir, if I ever...

HARDCASTLE: I tell you, she doesn't dislike you; and as

I'm sure you like her... I see no reason why you should not be joined as fast as the parson can tie you.

MARLOWE: But hear me, sir...

HARDCASTLE: Your father approves the match, I admire it; so there is no need for any delay.

MARLOWE: Why won't you hear me? I never gave Miss Hardcastle any hint to suspect me of affection. We had but one interview, and that was formal, modest, and uninteresting.

SIR CHARLES: And you never grasped her hand?

MARLOWE: As Heaven is my witness, I came down in obedience to your commands. I saw the lady without emotion, and parted without reluctance. And now I beg your leave of this house in which I have suffered so many mortifications. (*Exit.*)

SIR CHARLES: I'm astonished at his sincerity.

HARDCASTLE: And I'm astonished at the boldness of his denials.

SIR CHARLES: I'm certain my son is telling the truth.

HARDCASTLE: Here comes my daughter, and I would stake my life and honor upon her truth.

(Enter KATE.)

HARDCASTLE: Kate, come here, child. Answer us sincerely and without reserve: has Mr. Marlowe made you any professions of love and affection?

KATE: That is very abrupt question, sir. But since you require sincerity, Yes, he has.

HARDCASTLE: You see.

SIR CHARLES: And pray, madam, have you and my son had more than one interview?

KATE: Yes, sir, several.

HARDCASTLE: You see.

Sir Charles: But did he profess any affection?
Kate: Lasting affection.
Sir Charles: Did he talk of love?
Kate: Much, sir.
Sir Charles: Amazing!
Hardcastle: Now, my friend, I hope you are satisfied.
Sir Charles: And how did he behave, madam?
Kate: As most admirers do. He said some compliments about my face, talked of his lack of merit, and the greatness of mine; mentioned his heart, gave a short tragedy speech, and ended with pretended rapture.
Sir Charles: Now I'm perfectly convinced. I know his conversation among women to be modest and submissive: this can by no means be him. I am confident, he never did any such thing.
Kate: What if I should convince you? If you and my papa will place yourselves behind that screen, in about half an hour you shall hear him declare his passion to me in person.
Sir Charles: Agreed. And if I find what you describe then I don't know my own son. (*Exit.*)

Scene 3

The Garden at Night. Enter HASTINGS.

Hastings: What an idiot am I, to wait here for a fellow who takes a delight in mortifying me. I'm going to leave. He never intended to be punctual.

(Enter TONY, booted and spattered.)

Hastings: My honest squire! You are a man of your word and a true friend.

TONY: I'm your friend alright, and the best friend you have in the world, if you knew all I've through. This riding by night, by the way, is cursedly tiresome.

HASTINGS: Where did you leave your fellow-travellers? Are they in safe?

TONY: Twenty-five miles in two hours and a half is not such bad driving. The poor horses are done for.

HASTINGS: But where have you left the ladies? I dying with impatience.

TONY: Left them? Why where should I leave them but where I found them?

HASTINGS: This is a riddle.

TONY: Riddle me this then. What goes round the house, and round the house, and never touches the house?

HASTINGS: I... I don't know. What?

TONY: Why, that's it, man. I have led them astray. Egad, there's not a pond or a stream within five miles of the place but they know the taste of it.

HASTINGS: Oh, you took them in a round, while they supposed themselves going forward, and so you have at last brought them home again.

TONY: You shall hear it. I first took them down Feather-bed Lane, where we stuck fast in the mud. I then rattled them over the stones of Up-and-down Hill. I then led them on a circumbendibus path until I fairly lodged them in the horse-pond at the bottom of the garden.

HASTINGS: There wasn't an accident I hope?

TONY: No, no. Only mother is confoundedly frightened. She thinks she's forty miles off. She's sick of the journey; and the horses can scarce crawl. So if your own horses are ready, you may whip off with cousin, and I'll be bound there not a soul here can budge a foot to follow you.

HASTINGS: My dear friend, how can I ever thank you?

TONY: Ay, now it's "dear friend," "noble squire." Just now, it was all "idiot cub," and "run me through the guts." After we fight in this part of the country, we may kiss and be friends. But if you had run me through the guts, then I should be dead, and you might go kiss the hangman.

HASTINGS: I am most sorry. But I must hasten to relieve Miss Neville: if you'll keep the old lady employed, I promise to take care of the young one. (*Exit HASTINGS.*)

TONY: Never fear, here she comes. She's got in the pond, and is draggled up to the waist like a mermaid.

(Enter DOROTHY.)

DOROTHY: Oh, Tony, I'm killed! Shook! Battered to death. I shall never survive it. That last jolt has done me in.

TONY: Alack, mamma, it was all your own fault. You would be for running away by night, without knowing one inch of the way.

DOROTHY: I wish we were at home again. I never met so many accidents in so short a journey. Drenched in the mud, overturned in a ditch, jolted to a jelly, and on top of all to lose our way. Whereabouts do you think we are, Tony?

TONY: By my guess we have come upon Crackskull Common, about forty miles from home.

DOROTHY: O no! O no! The most notorious spot in all the country. We only want a robbery to make a complete disaster of it.

TONY: Don't be afraid, mamma, don't be afraid. Two of the five robbers that stayed here are hanged, and the other three may not find us. Don't be afraid. Is that a man that's galloping behind us? No; it's only a tree. Don't be afraid.

DOROTHY: The fright will certainly kill me.

TONY: Do you see anything like a black hat moving behind the thicket?

DOROTHY: Oh, death!

TONY: No; it's only a cow. Don't be afraid, mamma; don't be afraid.

DOROTHY: As I'm alive, Tony, I see a man coming towards us. Ah! I'm sure of it. If he sees us, we are undone.

TONY: Ah, it's a highwayman with pistols as long as my arm.

DOROTHY: Good Heaven defend us! He approaches.

Tony: Hide yourself, and leave me to manage him. If there is any danger, I'll cough. When I cough, be sure to keep hidden. (*DOROTHY hides behind a tree in the back scene. Enter HARDCASTLE.*)

HARDCASTLE: Unless I'm mistaken I heard voices of people in want of help. Oh, Tony! Is that you? I did not expect you so soon back. Are your mother and Miss Neville in safety?

TONY: Very safe, sir. (*Cough.*)

DOROTHY: (*From behind.*) Ah, death! there's danger.

HARDCASTLE: Forty miles in three hours. That's too much, my young fellow.

TONY: Stout horses and willing minds make short journeys. (*Cough.*)

DOROTHY: (*From behind.*) Surely he won't harm the dear boy.

HARDCASTLE: But I heard voices here. Is there someone else?

TONY: It was I, sir, talking to myself. I was saying that forty miles in four hours was very good going. (*Cough.*) To be sure it was. (*Cough.*) I have got a sort of cold by being out in the air. We'll go in, if you please. (*Cough.*)

HARDCASTLE: But even if you talked to yourself you did not answer yourself. I'm certain I heard two voices. I am resolved (*Raising his voice.*) to find the other out.

DOROTHY: (*From behind.*) Oh! he's coming to find me out. Oh!

TONY: Why do that, sir, if I've already told you? (*Cough.*) I'll lay down my life for the truth— (*Cough.*)—I'll tell you all, sir. (*Detaining him.*)

HARDCASTLE: I tell you I will not be detained. I insist on seeing.

DOROTHY: (*Running forward from behind.*) O lord! He'll murder my poor boy, my darling! Here, good gentleman, take your rage upon me. Take my money, my life, but spare that young gentleman; spare my child, if you have any mercy.

HARDCASTLE: Dorothy? Where did she come from? What is she talking about?

DOROTHY: (*Kneeling.*) Take compassion on us, good Mr. Highwayman. Take our money, our watches, all we have, but spare our lives. We will never bring you to justice; indeed we won't, good Mr. Highwayman.

HARDCASTLE: I believe she is out of her senses. Dorothy, don't you know me?

DOROTHY: Mr. Hardcastle, as I'm alive! My fears blinded me. But who... who could have expected to meet you here, in this frightful place, so far from home? What caused you to follow us?

HARDCASTLE: Dorothy, have you lost your wits? So far from home? You are within forty yards of your own door! (*To him.*) This is one of your old tricks, you graceless rogue. (*To her.*) Don't you know the gate, and the mulberry-tree; and don't you remember the horse-pond, my dear?

DOROTHY: Yes, I shall remember the horse-pond as long as I live. I almost caught my death in it. (*To TONY.*) And it is to you, you graceless scoundrel, I owe all this? I'll teach you to abuse your mother, I will.

TONY: Egad, mother, all the parish says you have spoiled me, and so now you are receiving the fruits of it.

DOROTHY: I'll spoil you, I will. (*Follows him off the stage.*)

HARDCASTLE: There is, however, truth and a moral in what he said. (*Exit.*)

(Enter HASTINGS and CONSTANCE)

HASTINGS: My dear Constance, don't delay. If we wait, all is lost. Pluck up a little resolution, and we shall soon be out of her reach.

CONSTANCE: I find it impossible. I'm so exhausted I simply cannot go on.

HASTINGS: Let us fly. Let us date our happiness from this very moment. Perish fortune! Love and contentment will increase what we possess beyond a king's ransom. Listen to me!

CONSTANCE: No, Mr. Hastings, no. Prudence must prevail. In the moment of passion fortune may be despised, but the time will come when passion is replaced by regret. I'm resolved to apply to Mr. Hardcastle's compassion and justice for redress.

HASTINGS: But though he had the will, he has not the power to satisfy your claims.

CONSTANCE: But he has influence, and I am going to rely on that.

HASTINGS: I have no hopes. But since you persist, I must reluctantly follow you.

Scene 4

The House. Enter SIR CHARLES and KATE.

SIR CHARLES: What a situation I am in! If what you say

appears, I shall then find a guilty son. If what he says is true, I shall then lose one that I most wished for a daughter.

KATE: I am pleased by your approval, and to show I merit it, if you place yourselves as I directed, I think you'll find satisfaction. Here he comes.

SIR CHARLES: I will fetch your father and bring him to the appointed place.

(Exit SIR CHARLES. Enter MARLOWE.)

MARLOWE: I'm preparing to leave but I had to come once more to see you. I did not, till this moment, know the pain I would feel in the separation.

KATE: (*In her own natural manner.*) I believe your sufferings cannot be so very great, sir, when you can so easily remove it. A day or two longer, perhaps, might lessen your uneasiness, by showing that perhaps I'm not that great a loss.

MARLOWE: That's not possible, madam. Every moment I spend with you my very pride begins to submit to my passion. The disparity between us in education and fortune, the anger of a parent, the contempt of my equals, all of these begin to lose meaning when I gaze into your eyes.

KATE: Then go, sir: I'll not try to detain you. Though my family be as good as hers you came down to visit, and my education, I hope, not inferior, what are these advantages without equal wealth? I must be contented knowing that you thought well of me even though your true aims are fixed on fortune.

(Enter HARDCASTLE and SIR CHARLES from behind.)

SIR CHARLES: Here, behind this screen.
HARDCASTLE: Aye, make no noise.
MARLOWE: By heavens, madam! Fortune was ever my smallest consideration. Your beauty at first caught my eye.

But every moment that I spend with you reveals some new grace. What seemed forwardness, now strikes me as courage and virtue.

SIR CHARLES: He amazes me!

HARDCASTLE: I told you how it would be. Hush!

MARLOWE: I am now determined to stay, madam; and I am certain once my father comes to really know you he will approve.

KATE: No, Mr. Marlowe, I will not, I cannot detain you. Do you think I could enter a permanent connexion where there was the smallest room for doubt? Do you think I would take advantage of a man's passing passion? Do you think I could ever relish my happiness if it was acquired at the expense of yours?

MARLOWE: I can have no happiness but what is in your power to grant me! The only regret I feel is not having seen your merits before. I will stay even contrary to your wishes.

KATE: Sir, please desist. Seriously, Mr. Marlowe, do you think I could ever submit to a connexion where I appear mercenary?

MARLOWE: (*Kneeling.*) Does this look like security? Every moment that shows me your merit, only serves to increase my love.

SIR CHARLES: I can hold it no longer. Charles, Charles, you have deceived me! Is this your indifference, your uninteresting conversation?

HARDCASTLE: Your cold contempt; your formal interview!

MARLOWE: What? What do you mean?

HARDCASTLE: You have one story for us, and another for my daughter.

MARLOWE: Daughter! This lady your daughter?

HARDCASTLE: Yes, sir, my only daughter; my Kate; whose else should she be?

MARLOWE: Oh.

KATE: Yes, sir, I'm also the tall squinting lady you met on your arrival (courtseying). You remember, the one you addressed as the mild, modest, sentimental man of gravity. Fortunately I later met the bold, forward, agreeable Rattle of the Ladies' Club.

MARLOWE: There's no bearing this; it's worse than death!

KATE: So, which is the real Marlowe? The faltering gentleman, who looks on the ground, and never sees my face; or the loud confident creature, that keeps it up with Mrs. Mantrap, till three in the morning? Ha! ha! ha!

MARLOWE: Curse my noisy head. I never meant to be impudent and yet... I must be gone.

HARDCASTLE: By the hand of my body, you shall not. I see it was all a mistake, and I am glad to find it so. You shall not leave, I tell you. I know she'll forgive you. Tell him you forgive him, Kate. We'll all forgive you. Take courage, man. (*They retire, she tormenting him, to the back scene.*)

(*Enter DOROTHY and TONY.*)

DOROTHY: So, they're gone off. Let them go. Good riddance.

HARDCASTLE: Who gone?

DOROTHY: My dutiful niece and her gentleman, Mr. Hastings, from town. He's the one who came down with our modest visitor here.

SIR CHARLES: My honest George Hastings? As worthy a fellow as lives. The girl could not have made a better choice.

HARDCASTLE: Then, by the hand of my body, I'm proud of the connexion.

DOROTHY: Well, he has taken away the lady, but he has not taken her fortune; that remains in this family to console us for her loss.

HARDCASTLE: Surely, Dorothy, you would not be so mercenary?

DOROTHY: That's my business, not yours.

HARDCASTLE: But you know if your son, when of age, refuses to marry his cousin, her whole fortune is then at her own disposal.

DOROTHY: True, but he's not of age, and she has not thought it proper to wait for his refusal.

(Enter HASTINGS and CONSTANCE.)

DOROTHY: What are you two doing here?

HASTINGS: (*To HARDCASTLE.*) For my attempt to fly off with your niece let my present confusion be my punishment. We are now come back, to appeal from your justice to your humanity. While her father was still living he gave permission for me to court his daughter.

CONSTANCE: Since his death, I have been obliged to stoop to deception to avoid oppression. I was ready to give up my fortune in order to secure my choice. But I am now determined to appeal to your tenderness to gain what is denied me.

DOROTHY: Nonsense, this is all but the whining end of a modern novel.

HARDCASTLE: Perhaps, but I'm glad they've come back. Come here, Tony. Do you refuse this lady's hand whom I now offer you?

TONY: What does it matter? You know I can't refuse her till I'm of age, father.

HARDCASTLE: While I thought concealing your age was likely to gain your improvement, I agreed with your mother's desire to keep it secret. But since I find she turns it to a wrong use, I must now declare you have been of age these three months.

TONY: Of age! Am I of age, father?

HARDCASTLE: And have been for three months.

TONY: In that case… (*Taking CONSTANCE's hand.*) Witness all men by these present, that I, Anthony Lumpkin, Esquire, of BLANK place, refuse you, Constantia Neville, spinster, of no place at all, for my true and lawful wife. So Constance Neville may marry whomever she pleases, and Tony Lumpkin is his own man again.

SIR CHARLES: Bravo!

HASTINGS: My worthy friend!

DOROTHY: My undutiful offspring!

MARLOWE: My dear George! I give you sincere joy. And could I prevail upon my little tyrant here to be less arbitrary, I should be the happiest man alive.

HASTINGS: (*To KATE.*) Come, madam, I know you like him, I'm sure he loves you, and you must and shall have him.

KATE: (*To MARLOWE.*) Sir, your "little tyrant" gladly concedes. Now you must be my agreeable Rattle.

HARDCASTLE: (*Joining their hands.*) And I say so too. Mr. Marlowe, if she makes as good a wife as she has a daughter, I don't believe you'll ever repent your bargain. So now to supper. To-morrow we shall gather all the poor of the parish about us, and the mistakes of this night shall be crowned with a merry morning. So, boy, take her; and as you have been mistaken in the mistress, my wish is, that you may never be mistaken in the wife.

Curtain

www.ingramcontent.com/pod-product-compliance
Lightning Source LLC
Chambersburg PA
CBHW030132100526
44591CB00009B/619